THE SPACE MY BODY FILLS

Books by Etta Blum

Poems (1937)

Translations from the Yiddish:
Revolt of the Apprentices:
Stories by Eliezer Blum-Alquit

Poems
Jacob Glatstein

THE SPACE
MY BODY FILLS

POEMS BY
Etta Blum

EXPOSITION PRESS   HICKSVILLE, NEW YORK

Acknowledgments

My thanks is extended to the Corporation of Yaddo, inexhaustibly, for the several fellowships which helped in the writing of these poems.

Several of the poems in this collection have previously been published.

"Encounter" © 1964 by The New York Times Company. Reprinted by permission.

"For Copland's Vitebsk" first appeared in *The Paris Review*, issue no. 34, Spring-Summer, 1965.

"St. Michael Slays the Devil" and "Red Roofs" first appeared in *Modern Occasions*, Spring 1971.

" 'Voice Has Two Shapes' " first appeared in *The Nation*, February 16, 1974, and the poem "I'm hard put" from the series "God: A Word" appeared in the March 8, 1975, issue.

The following were originally published in *Poetry*: "For Blake's Angels," April 1959; "Fog at Brighton," December 1963; "The Fountain, the Fire," August 1966; "Whatever it is I do" and "I am waiting," March 1967. The poems "Another Bird," "The Cave," "Your Final Anger," "City Park," "In Photograph Light" from the series "Words for Eli," appeared in the June 1965 issue.

"Aquarium Piece" first appeared in *The New Republic*, May 25, 1974.

First Edition

© 1959, 1963, 1965, 1966, 1967, 1971, 1974,
1975 by Etta Blum

ISBN 0-682-48265-X

Printed in the United States of America

*To my children,
Hannah and Frieda*

Contents

WORDS FOR ELI

FOR BLAKE'S ANGELS

THE SPACE MY BODY FILLS

Here in this room
there is only time and
the space my body fills.

I Cannot Recall Your Face,
Wherefore My True Loneliness

Under my eyelids
you start
        a cheek
your own eyelids
curving inward
               to
milk blue
All of me
        struggles
to see you together
I keep on fussing
with pieces
        Shall I
maybe
     better
take to
chipping from stone?

You Fell Asleep in the Park

I think birds
sleep like that
with dew-hung
feathers under
blanket of air
through the
shivery mid-hours
before dawn. Banked
against wind.
                    (Who
is it passes his
great granite hand
over the tops of
trees, ruffling
them like fur?)
                    The
sleep-caught silence
begins mostly with
gray, then turns
to summer green.

Aquarium Piece

The way the dolphin
moves, I'd like to go:
belly-about, face-all,
instructed tail and head
like keel and prow,
heart beating within
silences to glide
the precipiced flow.

In constant wheel the
dolphin goes, like
song returning to itself,
like cosmic thing or
wave or love that can-
not see impediment.

Its whiteness scarred
by what hostilities,
the dolphin does not
care but moves in
healing element more
swift than slow.

11

Zoo Piece: Rex Lion

Once seen, followed with sight
not wanting to comprehend
energy shouting from loins
without a dream of halt.

The walker circles a square
pace on pace more swift
carving a distance.

Copy the hammer motion
shuddering of iron limb.

Shag and fashioned pompom
decorate king and judge
shedding glorious fuss
on a most nakedness.

From the unopening lid
over look of gravity
hold self in frozen ambush.
Reflect on tyrannies
of man as beast: be glad
no recognition lights
those murderous marble eyes.

Fog at Brighton

Nothing has roots in the fog
Nothing grows from anything

The sky is full of moons
and everywhere is sky

Roofs open to smile

The distance to waves
breaking
is greater than surprise

Alone in the fog as
in the earth alone

Between the tall trash baskets
pigeons walk on the sand,
the bathers gone away

With myopic eyes we strain
and knock at memory
The ocean is not here

This Morning

for Alan Lelchuk

This morning was transfixion
before snow-tinselled pine,
wave of snowfield
glinting to sky.

The strange and the tender
will come to pass
as the seasons fall,
innocent of time,
of reckonings.

The vision of my crumbling
(animal born of my rib?)

                                                turns

toward me devoted
uncompassionate eyes.

All Day Was Twilight

All day was twilight
with fretted snow
blue
as of ducks' eggs.
The firs lit
with greenness,
tree trunks
darkdeep
propping the sky.
The sky's duck's blue!
There's no point
waiting
for a night
clutched tight by
budded day.
The lump that's Time
is in my throat.

In Water the Dream

The dream took place in water.
Inside of. That was to
mitigate recognition.
                        For
if I were to see you as
you were, I'd faint surely.
(Inside of a dream—faint?)
Anyhow, you loved me your
best on bed of blue
and sea-red—
Within the dream as
in water we
returned to what we were.
Wave curved your
cheek carefully to you.
Nothing else like—
If in water, I argued,
one can relinquish?
So my body, freed
of soul, exclaimed—
remembering.

Monkey You, You Harlequin

Monkey you, walking with
tenacious toes, barefoot
on sand, or dancing
                    go
How the gray sky throbs
with gray
            (to smoke and smudge)
unfolding, slashes blue
(so heart
            as infant
                        crows)
The calculation holds some-
where
        You are not here
or there (?)
                leaning on mist
with arms spread far
Comical your tears
                    (for shame!)
of relinquishment
                    O see,
death rides inside the wave
easily
        within reach
                    So
ankles dressed in white
ruffles of contented waves,
you Harlequin
                walk smiling
into water as in sleep . . .

Immersion

The secret. Inside of it.
Was there collusion?
My eyes reach to
your leaden rims where
you become sky as sky,
befogged.
       O my Atlantic,
my watery moon! How
you stretch limitless
limbs!
      Immersed
in your half-illumination,
my body buoyed by the
same weightlessness, I
float from crevasse
to crevasse. The circle
amazedly closes itself.

I swear to you: the guilt
and the suspicion
are quenched, all of it.
I am nothing now but
a listening.
        You'll
have no truck with words?
Still, I know well: it
is I whom you have chosen,
this time *me*.

Encounter

The Angel of the Night
greeted the Angel of the Day:
"Whatever happens in light
cannot equal the dream in sheer flight
that moves beneath the eyelid,
ghost-limbed and hid
within the mine of self,
thoughtlessly most itself."

The Angel of the Day replied:
"You know the truth of night
but the eye open to light
dreams no less far, though
with detail less bizarre.
The daydream is more stark,
spills feeling into the dark."

This was in that possible moment
of the hovering between;
neither angel was quite herself,
the one in just completion,
the other not yet begun.

God: A Word

1

I'm hard put:
the cloud by day,
the fire by night,
the voice from outer space.
Even the shower of gold.
You are not to be embraced,
most transparent of ghosts.
You come like a knocking,
like sun through lids.
I become light
with Being as you.

2

Whatever it is I do
I am praying.
That is a fact.
When I walk or eat or sleep,
something in me
holds its hands out
in supplication.
To what?
How should I know?
But the little altar
is set up neatly
and the prayer never tires
of saying itself.

3

I am waiting.
Through the dayhours
and the night. Some-
times the day is dark
and the night lightens
with sun. At times I
can hardly distinguish
the two, as from the same
parent sprung!
        Such confusion
and such clarity!
        The pigeon-
coo at dusk is equally to me
as dawnbirds singing. It
seems I have ears only
for these birds.
        For it
is they alone do not restrain
the blankness with which
I await, God, your word.

The Fountain, the Fire

The fountain, the fire,
the smoldering,
and the embrace of love.
I touched fingers lightly
to all of these.
I became a tree among the trees
(my leaves pretending to be wings)
and the birds played about me
before going to sleep.

I said to the birds:
"Who will tire first,
you or the fountain?"

I Am the Tree

I am the tree ascending.
At the topmost branch
I've become the bird,
starting from tip to
climb into above.
                    After-
ward, cloud.
                    Why not?
My purposes are clear.

Words for Eli

Why is thy countenance sad,
seeing thou art not sick?
This is nothing else but
sorrow of heart.

—King Artaxerxes to Nehemiah
Nehemiah 2:2

Another Bird

After a night when
my mind started hollow
with echoes; and the crowds,
intermittently passing
through the doorless rooms,
held up to me the occurrence
as a fruit grown to size,
with light and color
its own; when the past
became more present than
anticipation, I saw
the look of my hands
turning towards *me*
their appeal.
   That night
the edges of the past
shifted to roundness.
Daylight, unaccountably,
seeped in.
   It was then
that the bird (mine because
it was yours) sang quietly
into the stillness. The
city clamored, rang
raucous bells, outside

that circle of our stillness.

You are in the earth.
You are not warm nor cold.
Another bird chirps to you,
singing into the earth.

When the sun struck
our wall, it was a yellow
bursting.
              Too much brightness
for our bird. He flew
into a great dark leaf.

The New Dwelling

All the reins are loose,
my loss spills out over
the rims and into the
gutters, sloshes at the
curbs.
      To be without
you now is, as I foretold
once, to be with half my
soul.
      So crippled I hobble
from room to room, my
sadness running prodigally
through cracks of windowpanes.

Good luck! cry the people
from the rooftops. But
I can only hobble.

What am I doing here
without my old love
in a new place?

The Clock

Like an unseen wave, the
thought of your death
washes over me.
                    I am tipped,
go innerly screaming. The
clock starts burbling all
the mad sounds in one.

I know morning by light,
and I have marked off
the dark for night. Still,
I am uncertain about
these divisions.
                    On the
anniversary of your death
I shall light a candle
and try to curb my anger.

In Photograph Light

My imagination of your
death was like the
dream of my own, my
breath standing nearby.
The coffin with its
tenant (the face my own)
blurred and fogged,
made picture book.

How pleased my sadness
to see cascades of
tears in photograph
light. Through my imagined
choice.
       O wildly I
did not know, could
not prepare for this,
for your not-being,
for the brisk shoveling
of earth, for your
body blind as your eyes.

The Cave

Alone, I found the cave
where no cave was. Sat
on my haunches and gazed
into the point of darkness,
knowing posture of death.

But as yet, all I could
see was black on black.

I stared into that smudged,
that dotted darkness, saw
vapor swirling to fish, to
leaf, to blinded flower.

But never the face. Flut-
ter of eyelashes perhaps.

Lake of tears in my palm,
so straightly they fell.

Only when my shoulder moved
did my body follow after.

Your Final Anger

You told the doctor off:
I'm dying and you want
me to undress?
          With that
last angry look, yourself
completely, you turned and
died. You died then, angry
to your last breath. You
were yourself completely.
Death got no assent from
you. Like Moses, whom you
adored (and for that reason
partly) you would not agree.
And when you said "I'm dying"
you did not believe. You did
not, did you? It was your
way of threat. You've said
worse before, without dying.
This time, too, you didn't
really know. Else why the
anger?
        For this I love
you completely, for your
final anger. I knew if anger
couldn't save you, nothing could.

The Distance Lengthened

The doctor laid you
on the floor and ordered:
Breathe into his mouth.
With nearness sanctioned
(for I'd been fearful of
timidest touch) I knelt
and fitted lips to yours
and panted breath, how
zealously! bellows-like,
to search the doubtful
spark, even as a stranger
might (from having steeled
my longing and bidden
despair wait?)
            Too soon!
the glass of your eye
told me, the ruddiless
statue.
       Rising then,
I fled from unbelief,
walked away from your body
over threshold while
the distance between us,
gaping,
        lengthened
to marsh and precipice.

Good Night

I want to live with you
for a long time yet.

That was how you said good night
the night you died. I smiled
my blessings and my fear as
always.
          Omnipotent mother,
called upon to give you life,
I acceded. And for reward you
touched your lips to my neck,
brought me home again.
                              More
than your dying, it was
your passion not to die that
appalled me so.
              False mother,
I did not restrain your ebbing,
watched your blood leave its
stream and flow away. Secretly.

It was my task to keep you alive,
was it not? But how, my darling?
I cannot think how.
                Be good,
come to me in my dreams and
tell me now—*how?*

Now, What Shall I Do?

We came towards each other.
There was nothing could
stop it. It was our eyes
and our flesh sought each
other, and the best was done.
It was a happening like
other happenings in nature.
Not to be judged but accepted
with joy, with malediction
even, with whatever . . .

Now, what shall I do with
my dissatisfactions? Beneath
so much shovelled earth
you cannot be reached with
either love or torment.

I shall have to begin again
without you, like that
man with only half his
body, rolling himself on
a box down the street.

I Did Nothing Enough

After your death I
wasn't quiet enough.
I did not sit by your
body long enough.
                    I
did not wait for time
to fade of itself, but
arose and stepped into
interval. I read your
face, that is true. I
looked until my eyes
stopped seeing.
                    But still,
I did not look hard enough.
I could not match your
not-seeing.
                    Wanting to
comprehend, I said again
and again, *he is dead*,
to make me believe.
                    But
I did not believe enough.

The Unveiling

I listen to the message
of words in a language
I do not comprehend. They
go straight to the ears
of God and stir the scanty
grasses, so indifferently
planted. They probe beneath
the dirt to stir the dead
bones and the mouth with
the look of forever.
                    These
words say *all is well*, they
tell us to ask forgiveness
for the pain we caused you—
that which had meaning, and
that which had unmeaning. So
we ask forgiveness of you who
are nothing now, who are power-
less not to forgive.
                    Whatever
we say, humbly or unhumbly,
will have your assent, will
it not, dry bones and cold
flesh?
        I do not understand
the words, and perhaps in
any language they would
be incomprehensible?

Here is the stone, the
monstrous stone heavy unto
death, and the desultory
grass, unable to achieve
greenness.
  The words of
the preacher leap over the
trimmed bushes, the hunch-
backed bushes, ugly in
nature.
  No natural ground
this, where death is not
permitted its awfulness.

But I know the truth of
grayness, O Death,
in unanswering flesh.

City Park

My dear, it is no use.
You are within the earth.
And I, lying upon a knoll
in this city park, feel
your heart beating. So
much earth and life be-
tween. I see your smiles
and your angers, the
acceptance complete as
the rejection—so that
I scarcely know what to do.

Everything was possible.
It was your death was
the impossible thing.

Do you understand, now,
why I stared at your face
so endlessly?
           It was to
make certain that forever
after it would be everywhere.

The Remorse

All right. How was
I to know of your
childish disasters?
I who came to you
with my own? Needing
so much the strength
you flirted with?
So why didn't we
pool our disasters,
throw them down before
us like a pack of cards?
And shuffle and
reshuffle them?

My Refusal

I sat by your side and
waited. Searched your
dead eyes, with the light
glancing off them as
of dark pearl. The mouth
opened to soundlessness.
Yet I waited.
              Like a dumb
animal who had never heard
the word *death*, not
knowing how to say it.

My refusal waited, grew
to stubborn petals and
completely filled the room.

For Blake's Angels

About him were attendant seraphim, and each had six wings; one pair covered his face and one pair his feet, and one pair was spread in flight.

—Isaiah 6:2

Finishing Touches to a Portrait

for Fanny Glatstein

The artist bends to the canvas
to see what is to be seen
close by, withdraws to a distance,
brushes bouqueted in fist.
The head turns this way, that,
knowledge sweet in the eyes.
Wriggling paint on the palette
predicts the brightness
with which she extols the
dejected figure, making
identity more voluble.
With brushtip dares to touch
already created eyes and mouth.
She paints at arm's length,
wrist-length, finger-length,
and then retires to see
what must be seen from a distance.
Surely with the sight
of more than two eyes,
the agility of more
than ten fingers.

For Copland's Vitebsk

(with respects to Chagall)

He believes, he believes, the gray-eyed one
who puts your shards together.
(Cleft saucers are mended in Vitebsk.)
The brown-eyed one who patches your shoes
has limping fingers; his eyes too believe.
And the eyes of the flaxen-haired, the black-
braided, who move in a trance, making dainties
from wisps: delicate-limbed, they are grateful
for love on straw beds. All of the people in Vitebsk
are awry with tenderness—because all things
here believe. Even the threshold dust rises
upward.
        The lonely look out of windows
and forget their loneliness, seeing that
they too belong to Vitebsk. The babies sprawl
about until it is time to become *cheder* boys
when they will sit at rough tables learning
the *aleph-bes*. It's not two and two they are
putting together, it is God they are getting
to know.
        Everywhere in Vitebsk one hears
a speaking and a shouting and a whispering
to God. The houses flush and pale with the
knowledge. Piously the sun bounces over
the thatched roofs. In Vitebsk there is plenty
of sky. At night the moon is sad and sometimes
comical; there are two sides to this moon.

Sometimes, unsettled by so much belief,
the unbeliever walks into the hills
and stumbles among the stars, hears
the ram's horn stubborn in the night.

"Voice Has Two Shapes"

For Chinary Ung who tells how a
marauding band crossed the Vietnam
border into Cambodia in the dead
of night to ravage his hamlet.
He was two at the time.

Cradled in the crazed
one's arms, the child slept.
Fleeing from disaster, the
dream burst out of sleep.
Gunshot turned to firecrackers
in the childish brain. Red
slashed into black sky.
Cloudstuff rolled, orange
spilled into purple, spread.
In the stillness between,
teardrops glued, held by fog.
"Voice has two shapes?"
Nightmare slid to sunrise
as promise waterfalled.
Always after, the child
heard animal and angel song.

Red Roofs

(Soutine's)

All right, so it's *red roofs*
(my title too)
                a sort of orange-
red (you have to look for
it)
    but that's not
what started the thing.
                          It's
the way the houses are knocked
into each other,
                tangled
with trunks and leaf, the
windows slashed in
                    (any which
way)
    The whole thing
stuck together with wormy
green and yellow (pure)
                      and
blues in a frenzy.
                (The
torment's what's clear)
There's this feeling of
embrace
        (of Sabbath benediction
maybe) the branches leaning
towards each other
                  above
where the sky is, presumably.

I'd never been able to make
anything of it before
                    but *now*
I see how it's mine too,
I'm with it.
            The mishmash
speaks to me, that's how
I feel it.
            Like a place
under water maybe? Like
a drowning?
            We?

St. Michael Slaying the Devil

(Statue in wood by unknown
artist, South French, 15th
century, Brooklyn Museum)

The devil's upside down, St. Michael's dainty
foot poised on that uncouth shoulder. One horn
is gone, but that was not St. Michael's doing—
it was lost on a century.
                              The devil clutches
fast in either hand a leg of tiny
true believer who yet holds hands upright
in prayer. The devil dead or not, they'll go
on praying! (In the image of adults were they made.)

In his left hand St. Michael holds his shield,
for which he has no need since Heaven's with him.
His right hand's raised, thumb and forefinger circled
where the fateful spear was held (it too is gone)
which pierced right through the devil's upturned chin.
See how round and deep's the cleft it made!
It must have been a mighty spear to do
the trick, taller than St. Michael standing
tall in victory.
                      The devil's face
is broad and gross, teeth bared in rakish grin.
It seems he's not yet dead, but any moment
now—and the tiny martyrs will be freed!
St. Michael's tall and slim and angelrobed,
his face is long and thin as a saint's should be.
(A girl would wish to be as fair as he!)
Upon the clustered curls, that perfect bed,
it's clear the crown of sainthood has not budged.

St. Michael does not see the devil furious
at his feet; his gaze is heavenward.
(Good must not look at evil overlong,
just long enough to aim.)
                    Lovely St. Michael,
was it you who made that fatal thrust?
Could pretty nose and angel-look confound
the devil? (Perhaps, in the fifteenth century!)
Was there a passion in the act or was
it sweetness drove the spear?
                         This much we see:
St. Michael slew the devil once for all,
he pressed the devil down with his slim foot.

Notes at an Exhibition

for Rosemarie Beck

All of it, the pain
                    and
the delight that is
one kind of suffering
inside the stubby stroke
(they have to be this
way)
        and the dazzling
somberness
                (The reality
is the lovers', of that
we are certain)
                    the look
halted
        to flow forever?
Keats knew
                and knew
too the sumptuousness in
sand and tapestry of wave
the sky a linen
                    blue-white
This, the stuff of world
and love:
            (equally within
the room as on beach
or in woods)
            the frantic
grasp, the careful not-
touching
            (and after touch,
the tasting,
            the *delicates*

52

of *St. Agnes' Eve?*)
                              the
impossible tendernesses
                              with
everywhere the music too,
flowing
              The stand tells
us this, and piece of violin
buried within the pillow
(what else?)
                    Impossible
without music!
                    (*the hollow*
lute)
         The prodigality, the
need, the intolerable
consummation
                    is what it's for
There is this thing
                    between
Rosemarie and the face,
between Rosemarie and the
                                   body
between Rosemarie and
                              people
and the world.

Peridot Gallery, N.Y.
October 1966

A Chopper of Trees, This Maker of Music

for Gordon Binkerd

Before dawn and a while after
the birds sing madly in these woods.
They shun the dead trees (of which
there are so many) seeking the tipped
green and striped rose of sun.

Upon his bed in the cozy hut
within the forest where evergreen
live intimately with white birch
and maple, the maker of music
dreams wildly, stirs in his sleep.

Bird notes skip on his eyelids
no matter which way he turns,
drum the furrows of his brows.
When at last they reach to his
fingers, he awakens, stretching.

He sits at the piano and ponders.
It is his turn to make music now.
The hut sings, stilling the birds
who have never before heard such
sounds in these fortunate woods.

Will the hut grow wings and fly?
Birds hover at the window sills
(a window for each wall) peek in.
He is their good giant; at noon he
will throw them the queerest crumbs.

In the afternoon he becomes a
chopper of trees, this maker
of music; chooses the dead pine.
He knows it would take many life-
times to rid the forest of these,

but still, he does what he can.
Hearing the swoosh of his axe,
that sound in the air before
it goes *whack*, the birds flurry
away, their hearts on their wings.

The maker of music is proud
of his arm's swing, and his body
is held by the throw of the axe.
There is a time for music, he says,
and a time for the felling of trees.

114 Avenue of the Americas
(Facade facing Bryant Park)

> "Thou, silent form, dost tease
> us out of thought . . . "
> —*John Keats*

Concave start of stone
and glass
          (inverted wave)
falling to height
most singular. Mute worship-
pers, we search your root
in sky!
          (Your lap is sky)
Today is cloud on cloud,
the edges softer still
across a childhood's blue.
Tomorrow cataract eye
for soundless gray
                    (and
stars most winklessly)

Your lap is wave
                    (for
you are nothing
if not wave)
          You're
monument? You're
clue of waterfall?
               The
street's outdimmed, the
street's awash with you.

Tableau

On a certain spot in
the Cleveland Zoo
huge skulls of larger
animals—bison? deer?
lie scattered about
as adornment. And
for the entertainment
of smaller animals, birds
too. The way squirrels
run through porthole
eyes couldn't be more
inconsequent. Pigeons
march speculatively
through open mouths.
Stony, godcarved.
(The earth an August
dryness, the sky
sunned blue.) Although
these skulls speak
death in much the same
way, I do not even
think to think,
Poor Yorick!

The Machine as Hero
(Notes at an Exhibition)

> "I looked directly at the object
> and painted exactly what I saw."
> —*Walter Murch*

Me too. I'm telling you what I see.
Never mind it's the insides of the
Thermostat, the *Calculator*, the
Transformer
      secrets of a *Lock*—
the object uncluttered, yet
littered with the Beyond, a kind
of genesis, *yours*.
        Of course
the setup must be dramatic. If
an orange, a red ribbon, an onion—
why not? The shape's the thing.
"You can look at a thing so close
it ceases to be itself."
      Yes.
One can't look close enough to
see the way you saw it
      maybe
the way one comprehends your
seeing it. It adds up.
The mystery soldered to mystery.

Before the *Birthday Table*
(bemused)
     "The silver
got into everything."
      I saw
it before you told me, it
got on the tip of my nose
      even

my eyelashes. And the gold?
Moon Rock blasted with gold—
Moon? not electricity? not
light bulb?
                    Seeing the whitefish
in the window, you saw "gold, real
gold." Me too.
                    Your whitefish,
I mean.
              In case you don't know,
the gold got into everything
too
      the way the sea's in
the green cloth, skylight
caught into the folds
                        to vertigo
from looking long (and longer)
                                    What's
that you say, one thing's "almost
as good as another?"
                        So we come
to *Isotope, Carburetor, Car Heater*—
unaccountably the lemon, stubby
candle, a child's marble
                            "accessories"
merely (to be wary of meanings)
                                    So
journey to the interior of a
Clock
          iron cogs holding whatnot
together —
                Time? Time's what?

The *Wigheads*, ah, they *are!*
                                    Like-
wise the back of the doll's torso

(couldn't be *more* back)
                              one arm
unhinged at the elbow,
                        and *Fallen*
Cherub (alert) with doll eyes, head
and knee touching ground
                             upraised
middle wrapped in cloth of gold—
                                  "It
took her two years to fall that way?"
(provocatively)
                 So what's to see?
No nerves, no mess of lungs,
kidneys (nor heart)
                        trailing
corpuscles.
The mystery scuttled . . .
                     To get back
to the *Air Filter:* machine as hero
excels in element where color
moves
         (submerged seasons of a day)
and doth suffer a sea change . . .
                        Truly
your loaf of bread's "miraculous"
not freshly baked
                  more gold as rock
as jacket's stone. So forever, the
moment of forever
               (as fairy tale, as
ever after)
        As the *Two Doors*
couldn't be *flatter*
               but the colors
pop (something has to)

                    All of it
reminds of "other forms we
don't know about?"
                    The secret
in alarum of no-sound, in
round and breadth and apex—
                              cone,
cylinder, circle
                    you placing them
together, making offering
                    Still,
you kept on choosing the chipped
rock, the orange, the ribbon, the
green cloth—
          (*everyone's* biography?)
So? Nothing.
          I'm just saying.

"Dialogue" via earphone
Brooklyn Museum, January 1968

For Blake's Angels

Large as themselves the wings
of angels are; downfolded,
shoulder of wing looming
higher than shoulder of mortal;
to white gown's edge falling
the scalloped droop.

No rancor angels have
but show to the world
wondering eyes, the wish
large as their wings.
As crests of waves are
the longings of angels,
curling inward and lost.

Serenity their guerdon
won and worn as muted
eyelid over star.

So move with dignity
and seldom actually fly.

Into such solemn company
how can I go with turned-
down heels and headlong woe?